AF359775

d for dama
ion contaii

ill also g

spect me

ıs grow.

ches us t

ome unf

gs to wai

to talk.

ne to car

ature is (

s treat u

et anyone

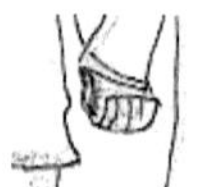

ill remen
with som

erson wl

erson wl

d to the

thing it .

nany thi

orries ge

lets our l

s keeps u

;ome pai

f beautif

m we do r

uncondi

ill that p

's till the

LITTLE
SISTER

are divi

. you whe

ul it ma

*for disa

promise

after sun

:o learn r

hday tod

me.

forget th

ı *helps u.*

; *it has*

way

r powers

e a family

e educatic

*did my j
mentor.*

a person